planet earth

INCREDIBLE REPTILES

By Tracey West

SCHOLASTIC INC.

New York   Toronto   London   Auckland   Sydney
Mexico City   New Delhi   Hong Kong

Photo Copyright Credits

Cover: Stephen Alvarez / National Geographic Stock. Title page: Jonathan Ayres / Alamy. Page 1: Eky Chan / Shutterstock (top left): Claus Meyer / Minden Pictures. Page 2: Georgette Douwma / Photographer's Choice / Getty Images. Page 3 (clockwise from top): Nicole Duplaix / National Geographic Stock; Michael & Patricia Fogden / Minden Pictures; Stephen Dalton / Minden Pictures; Daniel Heuclin / NHPA / Photoshot; ZSSD / Minden Pictures. Page 4: James Gerholdt / Peter Arnold Inc. Page 5: Biosphoto / Crocetta Tony / Peter Arnold Inc. Page 6: BBC Planet Earth / Tom Brakefield / Digital Vision. Page 7: M.Gunther / BIOS / Peter Arnold Inc. Pages 8-9: Page 10: BIOS / Peter Arnold Inc. Page 11: Jim Merli / Visuals Unlimited, Inc. Page 12 George McCarthy / CORBIS. Page 13:Alex Hibbert / Alamy. Page 14: Michael & Patricia Fogden / Minden Pictures. Page 15: Brian P. Kenney / Animals Animals. Pages 16-17: Tim Flach / Stone / Getty Images. Page 18: Doug Cheeseman / Peter Arnold Inc. Page 19: David M. Dennis / Animals Animals. Page 20:Zigmund Leszczynski / Animals Animals.Page 21:Marian Bacon / Animals Animals. Pages 22-23: Biosphoto / Monchâtre Robin / Peter Arnold Inc. Page 24: Bob Blanchard / Shutterstock. Page 25: Audrey Snider-Bell / Shutterstock. Page 26: Timothy Laman / National Geographic / Getty Images. Page 27: Superstock / Photolibrary. Page 28: Thomas Marent / Minden Pictures. Page 29: Gregory G. Dimijian, M.D. / Photo Researchers. Page 30: Martin Harvey / Alamy. Page 31: Fred Bavendam / Minden Pictures. Pages 32-33: Adam White / NPL / Minden Pictures. Page 34: rf from BBC Planet Earth / Photodisc. Page 35: SA Team / Minden Pictures. Pages 36-37: Tom Brakefield / Corbis. Page 38: Paul Souders / Corbis. Page 39: Robert Maier / Animals Animals. Page 40: Vassil Donev / epa / Corbis. Page 41: © Maik Dobiey / Cal Photos. Pages 42-43: Tom & Pat Leeson. Page 44: David Northcott / Danita Delimont / Alamy. Page 45: © Jacob Dulisse

ISBN-13: 978-0-545-11413-4

ISBN-10: 0-545-11413-6

BBC (word mark and logo) are trademarks of the British Broadcasting Corporation and are used under license.

Planet Earth logo © BBC 2006. BBC logo © BBC 1996.

BBCEARTH is a trademark of the BBC

Published by Scholastic Inc.

SCHOLASTIC and associated logos are trademarks and/or registered trademarks of Scholastic Inc.

12 11 10 9 8 7 6 5 4 3 2 1   9 10 11 12 13 14/0

Printed on paper containing minimum of 30% post-consumer fiber.

Printed in the U.S.A.

First printing, August 2009

CONTENTS

A WORLD OF REPTILES

There are 8,000 different species of reptiles on planet Earth. What makes a reptile a reptile?

This class of animals has these things in common:

- They are cold-blooded. That means their body temperature is controlled by the environment around them.
- They breathe air.
- They are vertebrates (have a backbone).
- They have tough skin covered with scales.
- Most lay eggs—some snakes give birth to live young.

REPTILE GROUPS

Reptiles living today can be divided into four major groups:

1 Turtles: including tortoises and terrapins

2 Lizards and snakes

3 Crocodilians: including alligators, caimans, and crocodiles

4 Tuataras: lizard-like species that belong to an ancient group of reptiles from the Triassic Period

THE LANDSCAPES OF THE EARTH

All reptiles live in one of these landscapes:

FRESH WATER

Earth is a planet filled with water—but only 3 percent of it is fresh. All organisms need fresh water to survive, including fish, birds, reptiles, amphibians, and other mammals that live in the world's lakes, rivers, and streams.

GREAT SANDS

The blazing hot temperatures of the world's deserts make it difficult for any kind of life to survive. The animals that do live there have developed their own strategies to get food and water.

RAINFOREST

In rainforests, the mix of sun and rain provides the perfect conditions for plants to thrive—and provides a rich habitat for all kinds of life.

SHALLOW SEAS

These regions of shallow water surround each of the continents. They are a small part of the world's oceans, but contain rich areas of life, including coral reefs and forests of seaweed.

OPEN OCEAN DEPTHS

Some of the planet's most mysterious creatures live deep in the ocean, beyond where humans can travel.

GREAT PLAINS

Animals thrive on these large, grass-covered plains, which are found in every continent except Antarctica.

MOUNTAIN HEIGHTS

Mountain-dwelling animals must endure high altitudes and temperatures that range from hot to extreme cold.

YELLOW ANACONDA

AVERAGE WEIGHT	**AVERAGE LENGTH**	**WHERE IT LIVES**	**FAVORITE FOODS**
40 pounds	10–15 feet	rivers, lakes and swamps in Bolivia, Argentina, Paraguay, and Brazil	large rodents, caiman, birds, fish, and turtles

The yellow anaconda is smaller than the green anaconda. They have either dark brown or blue markings covering a yellow body.

DiD You Know?

A female yellow anaconda can give birth to 24 or more babies at once, before leaving the small snakes on their own to survive.

GREEN ANACONDA

AVERAGE WEIGHT
330 pounds

AVERAGE LENGTH
about 20 feet

WHERE IT LIVES
tropical rainforests, swamps, marshes, and streams in South America

FAVORITE FOODS
wild pigs, deer, capybara, birds, turtles, and caimans

Open wide! Stretchy ligaments in the jaw allow this reptile to swallow its prey whole.

SPECTACLED CAIMAN

Also Known As: Common caiman, Tinga

AVERAGE LENGTH	**WHERE IT LIVES**	**FAVORITE FOODS**
3–6 feet	rivers, wetlands, and rainforests in Central America	fish, amphibians, reptiles, water birds, and wild pigs

DiD You Know?

A bony ridge between the eyes gives this croc its name. It makes its eyes look as if they are connected like eyeglasses.

MUGGER CROCODILE

Also Known As: Crocodile of the marsh, Indian swamp crocodile

AVERAGE LENGTH	WHERE IT LIVES	FAVORITE FOODS
about 14 feet	freshwater in Bangladesh, India, Iran, Nepal, Pakistan, and Sri Lanka	crustaceans, fish, insects, snakes, turtles, birds, and deer

These reptiles love to inhabit wet, swampy areas. The mugger will travel long distances to find water.

NILE CROCODILE

AVERAGE WEIGHT	AVERAGE LENGTH	WHERE IT LIVES	FAVORITE FOODS
500–2000 pounds	15–16 feet	lakes, rivers, and marshes in Africa south of the Sahara	flsh, zebras, small hippos, antelope, warthogs, porcupines, wildebeest, birds, other crocodiles, and carrion

Thick, horny scales and bony plates on the nile crocodile's back protect this animal from predators such as lions.

DiD You Know?

If a nile crocodile can't finish its meal, it saves the leftover pieces underwater for later.

The crocodile can't chew. Instead, it tears chunks from its prey by twisting its body. This is called the death roll. To swallow food, it tips its head back.

GIANT AMAZON RIVER TURTLE

Also Known As: Arrau

AVERAGE WEIGHT
females can weigh up to 200 pounds

AVERAGE LENGTH
the shell of a female can reach up to 40 inches

WHERE IT LIVES
rivers in South America

FAVORITE FOODS
fruits, leaves, seeds, crabs, fish, shrimp, and dead fish

The giant Amazon River turtle belongs to the side-necked family of turtles. These turtles turn their heads to the side to hide them underneath the shell.

SNAPPING TURTLE

AVERAGE WEIGHT
between about 8 and 35 pounds

AVERAGE LENGTH
between about 7 and 18 inches

WHERE IT LIVES
lakes, ponds, rivers, and streams in Canada and the United States

FAVORITE FOODS
carrion, leaves, algae, invertebrates, and any small mammals and amphibians it can catch

To communicate, snapping turtles face each other and make movements with their legs.

DiD You Know?

Adult snapping turtles don't have many predators. But they will sometimes fight each other. The fights can end with one turtle biting off the head of another.

AMERICAN ALLIGATOR

AVERAGE WEIGHT
from about 450 to up to 1,000 pounds

AVERAGE LENGTH
13–18 feet from head to tail

WHERE IT LIVES
warm wetlands and swamps in states in the southeast United States

FAVORITE FOODS
lizards, fish, snakes, turtles, crustaceans, small mammals, birds

The alligator's tail is about the same length as its body. The tail is used for swimming, as a weapon, and to dig holes.

CHINESE ALLIGATOR

Also Known As: Yangtzee alligator

AVERAGE WEIGHT	AVERAGE LENGTH	WHERE IT LIVES	FAVORITE FOODS
up to 88 pounds	between 4 ½–6 feet	rivers, lakes, streams, ponds, and swamps in Central China	fish, snails, clams, rats, and ducks

DiD You Know?

You've probably heard of a lion's roar, but reptiles roar too. Some crocodilians, like the Chinese alligator, will roar loudly to scare off intruders.

This alligator's teeth are good for crushing the hard shells of the clams and other mollusks this alligator eats.

SHOVEL-SNOUTED LIZARD

AVERAGE LENGTH	WHERE IT LIVES	FAVORITE FOODS
about 4 inches	in the deserts of Africa, from Western Namibia to southwest Angola	plants, seeds, and insects

This lizard gets its name from its flat snout. It uses it to dig into the sand to escape the desert heat. When it gets hungry, it digs back up to the surface.

DiD You Know?

The lizard does a kind of dance to get across the hot sand. It only lifts up one of its front feet and one of its hind feet at a time. It uses its tail for support.

PERINGUEY'S SIDEWINDING ADDER

Also Known As: Peringuey's viper, the sidewinding adder

AVERAGE LENGTH
8–10 inches

WHERE IT LIVES
the Namib desert in southwest Africa

FAVORITE FOODS
lizards

This snake's eyes are located at the top of its head, helping the adder to hunt. It buries its body in the sand, with only its eyes and tip of the tail sticking out.

GILA MONSTER

AVERAGE WEIGHT	AVERAGE LENGTH	WHERE IT LIVES	FAVORITE FOODS
up to 3.25 pounds	16–20 inches	deserts in the southwestern United States and northern Mexico	eggs, lizards, small birds, and rodents

When the weather is warm, the gila monster stores extra fat in its lower body and tail. Like many reptiles, this lizard goes into a hibernation-like state in the winter. That's when it draws on this stored-up energy.

The gila monster has poisonous venom. It flows through the teeth in its lower jaw. The poison enters the victim when the lizard chews on it.

DiD You Know?

It's unusual to see more than one gila monster at a time in the wild. These lizards like to live alone.

RAINFOREST
CARPET PYTHON

AVERAGE LENGTH	WHERE IT LIVES	FAVORITE FOODS
6½–12 feet	rainforests in Australia and New Guinea	small and medium-sized mammals, birds, and lizards

Did You Know?

The carpet python spends most of its time on the forest floor, looking for small animals to eat. In the rainforest, carpet pythons also spend time in the trees, and will even lay their eggs in tree hollows.

BROWN TREE SNAKE

AVERAGE LENGTH
from about
3–6 ½ feet

WHERE IT LIVES
mangrove forests and swamps in Indonesia, Australia, the Solomon Islands, New Guinea, and Guam

FAVORITE FOODS
birds, lizards, and mammals

This snake is active at night and spends its days coiled in a cool, dark spot, such as a treetop. They are great climbers.

GREEN TREE MONITOR

Also Known As: Emerald monitor

AVERAGE LENGTH	WHERE IT LIVES	FAVORITE FOODS
about 3 feet	forests and mangrove swamps in Australia and New Guinea	insects including grasshoppers, roaches, beetles, centipedes, and spiders; crabs, and bird eggs

This lizard has a prehensile tail. That means its tail can wrap around things. The green tree monitor uses this long tail to help it climb trees.

GECKO

AVERAGE LENGTH	WHERE IT LIVES	FAVORITE FOODS
almost 10 inches from head to tail	rainforests in the north of Madagascar	insects

On the bottom of the gecko's feet are tiny cells shaped like hooks. These help the gecko cling to smooth surfaces.

DiD You Know?

When this gecko is being chased by a predator, it has an escape plan. It can break off its tail! A new tail will grow back, but it's usually shorter with a different pattern.

GREEN IGUANA

AVERAGE WEIGHT	AVERAGE LENGTH	WHERE IT LIVES	FAVORITE FOODS
11 pounds	6.5 feet	rainforests in Mexico, Central America, the Caribbean Islands, and Brazil	leaves, flowers, and fruit

This loose flap of skin under the throat is called a dewlap. The iguana can extend the dewlap to absorb heat or to scare off an enemy.

Did You Know?

Iguanas like to live in the branches of trees where there are plenty of leaves and fruit to eat. If a predator attacks, they will jump from their perch and land in the water below. They're excellent swimmers.

CUBAN BROWN ANOLE

Also Known As: Mayan coastal anole

AVERAGE LENGTH
up to 8.5 inches

WHERE IT LIVES
Cuba, the Caribbean Islands, Florida, Georgia, and Hawaii

FAVORITE FOODS
arthropods, annelis, and mollusks

The color of an anole's skin can change in just a few minutes.

TOKAY GECKO

AVERAGE LENGTH	WHERE IT LIVES	FAVORITE FOODS
14 inches	rainforests, cliffs, and trees in southeast Asia	insects

Did You Know?

This gecko's ears are located in small holes on either side of the head. If you look through one hole, you can see clear through to the other side!

RETICULATED PYTHON

AVERAGE WEIGHT	AVERAGE LENGTH	WHERE IT LIVES	FAVORITE FOODS
up to 300 pounds	up to 30 feet	rainforests, woodlands, and grasslands in the Philippines, Indonesia, southeastern Asia, and Pacific Islands	mammals, birds, lizards, and snakes

Female reticulated pythons lay eggs. Then they coil their body around the eggs to keep them warm and protected.

KING COBRA

Also Known As: Hamadryad cobra

AVERAGE WEIGHT	AVERAGE LENGTH	WHERE IT LIVES	FAVORITE FOODS
up to 20 pounds	12–16 feet	rainforests and mangrove swamps in India, southern China, and southeast Asia	other snakes, frogs, and lizards

The neck flaps on a King Cobra are called the "hood." The hood flares out to scare prey or frighten off a predator.

DiD You Know?

This snake doesn't have the strongest poison in the world—but one dose of this poison is enough to kill more than 20 humans, or one Asian elephant.

AVERAGE LENGTH OF ADULT MALES	WHERE IT LIVES	FAVORITE FOODS
12–17 inches	forests in Madagascar	insects, small birds, and other reptiles

Depending on where they live in Madagascar, the color of this chameleon ranges from green to blue to red.

DiD You Know?

The panther chameleon drinks by licking the dew off of leaves.

MADAGASCAN TREE BOA

AVERAGE LENGTH	WHERE IT LIVES	FAVORITE FOODS
up to 8 feet	in low and mountainous forests in Madagascar	small mammals and birds

Heat-sensitive pits around the boa's mouth help it find prey. This also allows the boa to hunt in the dark.

SALTWATER CROCODILE

AVERAGE WEIGHT
from about 880 pounds to more than 2200 pounds

AVERAGE LENGTH
adult males can reach up to 20 feet

WHERE IT LIVES
in coastal waters and some freshwater habitats in Australia and Asia

FAVORITE FOODS
crustaceans, turtles, lizards, birds, and sometimes larger mammals such as buffalo, livestock, wallabies, wild boar, and monkeys

Reaching lengths of 20 feet or more, this is the largest member of the crocodilian family.

BANDED SEA KRAIT

Also Known As: Yellow-lipped sea krait

AVERAGE LENGTH
adult females can reach up to 50 inches

WHERE IT LIVES
waters around the coast of New Guinea, the Philippines, Sri Lanka, southeast Asia, Japan, and the Pacific Islands

FAVORITE FOODS
eels and small fish

Large scales on the belly allow these snakes to move on land.

DiD You Know?

The venom of a banded sea krait is ten times more powerful than rattlesnake venom! Fortunately, they rarely attack humans, even if they feel threatened.

ALDABRA GIANT TORTOISE

AVERAGE WEIGHT
350 pounds for females, and more than 550 pounds for males

AVERAGE LENGTH OF SHELL
3 feet for females, 4 feet for males

WHERE IT LIVES
the nation of Seychelles, a small group of islands north of Madagascar

FAVORITE FOODS
plants

When the only water around is in shallow puddles, the tortoise will drink through its nostrils to get as much water as possible.

DiD You Know?

Like all reptiles, the aldabra tortoise needs to bask in the sun to warm up its body temperature. But the islands these tortoises call home can get brutally hot. So the tortoises wake up early to eat, and then hurry back to the shade before the scorching midday heat strikes.

GREEN TURTLE

Also Known As: Green sea turtle

AVERAGE WEIGHT	AVERAGE LENGTH	WHERE IT LIVES	FAVORITE FOODS
300-500 pounds	3 feet or more	open ocean and coastal habitats in the tropics and subtropics	seagrass and algae

A hard shell helps protect this turtle from predators.

DiD You Know?

Adult green turtles are the only sea turtles that eat only plants. Their plant-based diet may be what turns the fat under the shell a greenish color.

LEATHERBACK TURTLE

AVERAGE WEIGHT
up to an average
of 2000 pounds

AVERAGE LENGTH
up to an
average of
6 feet

WHERE IT LIVES
open ocean and coastal
habitats around the world.
They nest in parts of South
America and Africa

FAVORITE FOODS
mostly jellyfish,
but also squid,
crustaceans, fish,
algae, and seaweed

Other sea turtles have a hard shell, but this turtle's shell
is made of leatherlike tissue. The shell has ridges in it and
tapers in the back.

EGYPTIAN COBRA

Also Known As: Egyptian asp

AVERAGE LENGTH	WHERE IT LIVES	FAVORITE FOODS
6 feet	steppes, savannas, and semi-deserts in North Africa and the Middle East	rodents, frogs, toads, and birds

DiD You Know?

Like many snakes, the venom of the Egyptian cobra is a neurotoxin. That means it is a poison that attacks the nervous system of the victim.

The cobra's fangs are hollow to hold venom.

FLAT LIZARD

WHERE IT LIVES
savanna and
rocky areas in
South Africa

FAVORITE FOODS
black flies and
figs

The colors on top of the body are
duller than those underneath.
This is so the lizards don't
draw attention to birds
or other predators
overhead.

DiD You Know?

Males of this species sport
bright colors including shades of blue
and turquoise,
yellow, and orange.

EUROPEAN LEGLESS LIZARD

Also Known As: Glass lizard

AVERAGE WEIGHT	AVERAGE LENGTH	WHERE IT LIVES	FAVORITE FOODS
11–21 ounces	2-3 feet from head to tail	dry habitats in Europe and Asia	small mammals, bird eggs, worms, insects, and earthworms

Although it has no legs, this lizard does have a small "stump" where its back legs would be.

Did You Know?

This reptile is a lizard, not a snake. You can tell by looking at its head. It has movable eyelids and holes for ears—something lizards have, but snakes don't.

BLACK MAMBA

AVERAGE WEIGHT	AVERAGE LENGTH	WHERE IT LIVES	FAVORITE FOODS
up to 3.5 pounds	about 8 feet	savannas and rocky hillsides in southern and eastern Africa	rodents, bats, birds, and lizards

These snakes won't attack unless they feel threatened. Each bite is packed with powerful venom. A human will usually die 20 minutes after being bitten by the black mamba unless antivenin is used.

ASHE'S SPITTING COBRA

Also Known As: Brown spitting cobra

AVERAGE LENGTH	WHERE IT LIVES	FAVORITE FOODS
up to 9 feet or more	dry lowlands in Kenya, Uganda, and Ethiopia	eggs, carrion, snakes, lizards, and birds

Did You Know?

If danger approaches, the cobra can spit its venom as far as 6½ feet! It aims for the eyes. The venom blinds the attacker for a short time—enough time for the spitting cobra to escape.

VEILED CHAMELEON

Also Known As: True chameleons

AVERAGE LENGTH OF ADULT MALE
17 to 24 inches

WHERE IT LIVES
in the mountain regions of Yemen, the United Arab Emirates, and Saudi Arabia

FAVORITE FOODS
insects

The eyes can look in two different directions at once and swivel around nearly 180 degrees. This means the chameleon can follow prey with its eyes while keeping its body completely still.

DiD You Know?

Chameleons are known for their ability to change color. The color changes are most often used for emotions, but also for temperature changes and camouflage.

JACKSON'S CHAMELEON

AVERAGE LENGTH
between about 9 and 21 inches long

WHERE IT LIVES
in trees in the mountains of East Africa

FAVORITE FOODS
insects, worms, and other invertebrates

You will always see three horns on a male Jackson's chameleon. Females don't always have them.

WESTERN SKINK

AVERAGE LENGTH
up to almost
8 inches, but
usually smaller

WHERE IT LIVES
in woodlands, pine forests,
and areas near and away from
water in the western United
States and parts of Canada

FAVORITE FOODS
insects such as crickets,
beetles, flies, and
grasshoppers; spiders,
and earthworms

Smooth, curved scales
make this lizard look shiny.

DiD You Know?

When a skink is young, its
tail is a brilliant shade of
blue. As the skink gets older,
the blue color fades.

GLOSSARY

Antivenin: something that stops the harmful effects of snake poison

Camouflage: a protective coloring that helps an animal hide in its environment

Carrion: the rotting body of a dead animal

Coastal: land that is near water, such as the ocean

Crustacean: a group of water-dwelling animals that don't have backbones, but have a hard shell and jointed limbs

Habitat: the place where an animal lives

Ligament: strong tissue that connects the bones in the body

Predator: an animal that hunts other animals for food

Prey: an animal that is killed and eaten by other animals

Species: a group of animals or other organisms that have the same characteristics and can breed with each other

Vertebrate: an animal with a backbone

PROTECT PLANET EARTH

It's the Only One We've Got . . .

Here's a Bright Idea! If you're leaving a room for more than 30 seconds, flip the switch. You'll save energy—and reduce your energy bill, too!

Buy Recycled. Encourage your parents to buy recycled paper products for your house.

Reusable Containers Rule. When it comes to your lunch, the less packaging, the better. Individually wrapped snacks and drinks waste resources. Instead, use reusable containers from home to bring your food to and from school.

Down the Tubes. Why not turn off the faucet when you're brushing your teeth? You'll save lots of water from going down the drain.

Put Your Computer to Sleep. Using a screensaver on your computer uses more energy than if you let it go to sleep. So change the preferences on your computer and give it a rest.

Bring Your Own Bag. If you're going shopping, bring your own reusable bags with you. Plastic bags are made from petroleum (aka oil) and paper bags are made from trees. So if you bring your own reusable bag, you won't be wasting either!

Recharge Your Batteries. Buy rechargeable batteries that you can reuse, rather than disposable batteries that you throw away.

Remember the Three R's. Reduce. Reuse. Recycle. These are important ways to cut down on consumption and waste.